ba

Printed and bound in Great Britain by MPG Books Limited, Bodmin,
Cornwall

Published by SMT, an imprint of Sanctuary Publishing Limited, Sanctuary
House, 45-53 Sinclair Road, London W14 0NS, United Kingdom

www.sanctuarypublishing.com

ISBN: 1-84492-035-6

basic Bass Workout

Stuart Clayton

smt

CONTENTS

FOREWORD

I hope you enjoy this book – I certainly enjoyed putting it together for you. The aim is to introduce you to some new techniques and to teach you a little about the history of our favourite instrument. I also hope that I've been able to present some music theory to you in a sensible manner and one that you can understand. If, however, you have any questions or comments, you can reach me through my website, www.stuartclayton.co.uk – I will do my best to help!

Stuart Clayton
Spring 2004

INTRODUCTION

No doubt you already know that playing the bass, or indeed any instrument, can be a very rewarding experience. You probably also know that at other times it can be extremely daunting and frustrating. With so many styles, techniques and songs out there, it's often difficult to know what to focus on, what to learn and, more importantly, what to play. If this sounds familiar, then this book is for you, because my aim is to help you understand all those aspects and how and when to apply them.

As with any instrument, you'll get out of the bass what you put in. The more time you spend honing your craft, the better at it you will become. There will be some hard work ahead, but that doesn't mean it can't be enjoyable. Practice is the key to your success, and with enough of it you can do anything you like. Keep that in mind when things get tough.

Finally, this isn't one of those books that you're meant to read from cover to cover. You can if you want, but I don't recommend it. The idea is that you dip into it when you want to know something. The information is here to be digested at your leisure as and when you want it. Whatever you do, enjoy it.

1 TUNING UP

Before you tune up, you must always have something that will provide you with an accurate reference pitch – unless you're lucky enough to have perfect pitch! Assuming that you don't, a reference pitch can be either a keyboard (or other instrument that is reliably in tune) or an electronic guitar tuner. An electronic tuner is an excellent purchase for any bassist/guitarist, as it is never wrong and will enable you to tune up on stage without amplifying the bass. A tuner such as this can be purchased from your local music shop for as little as £15 ($23).

Warning! Tuning without a reference pitch can result in an instrument that's in tune with itself but not with anything else – not much good for playing with other musicians!

There are a couple of good ways of tuning the bass, which I will illustrate for you here. Both are accepted methods and it really doesn't matter which one you end up using.

Method 1

Firstly, make sure you have the top string (G) of your bass in tune before proceeding any further.

Now play the open G string and the fifth fret of the D string – also a G. Both positions should produce the same pitch.

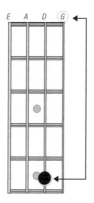

If the pitches are not identical, adjust the D string's tuning key until they are. Here's a particularly important point: make sure that you adjust the correct tuning peg. If you accidentally adjust the G-string tuning peg, your only in-tune string will now be out of tune!

basic Bass Workout

The next two diagrams illustrate how to get the rest of the strings in tune. Repeat the previous process with the open D string and the fifth fret on the A string. Again, both should produce the same pitch – in this case, a D.

Once more, repeat the process with the open A string and the fifth fret on the E string. Both should produce the same pitch – an A.

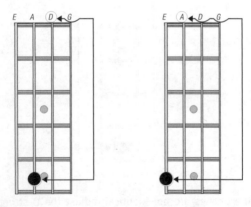

The bass should now be in tune. Try playing a few lines to see how it sounds. If anything sounds amiss, check each note pairing as illustrated to find the fault. Bear in mind that small mistakes are cumulative and will be even more obvious by the time you finish tuning!

Method 2

Method 2 is another very commonly used method for tuning and is for the slightly more advanced player. It is similar to Method 1 except that it uses harmonics. Harmonics are played by placing a finger over the fret without pushing it down and then playing the string. This will produce a bell-like tone that is above the usual bass register. One of the advantages of using this method is that you don't need to keep your finger on the string to keep the harmonic ringing, enabling you to have your left hand free to manipulate the tuning peg. I find this method of tuning more accurate than the previous one. You will see why shortly.

As before, you must ensure that you have the G string in tune before tuning the other strings. Once you're happy with the tuning of your G string, play the harmonic at the seventh fret on the G string and the harmonic at the fifth fret on the D string. They should be identical.

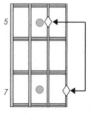

basic Bass Workout

If the harmonics aren't in tune with each other, you'll
hear a 'pulse' in the sound, a movement that slows
down the closer towards being in tune the two notes
become. If you can hear this pulsing, slowly tune
upwards or downwards until the pulsing is inaudible.
This is the main advantage this method has over the
first. For those of you who play five-string basses, you'll
find it much easier to tune up that difficult low B string
using this method.

Next repeat the procedure down a string, playing the
harmonic at the seventh fret on the D string and the
fifth fret on the A string. Again, they should be
identical:

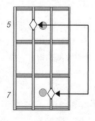

And again with the seventh fret on the A string and the
fifth fret on the E string:

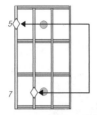

Your bass should now be in tune. Check for inconsistencies and correct them as necessary. Again, be careful to get each string right as you go, as small mistakes add up!

2 LEARNING THE FRETBOARD

Without a good understanding of where the notes are on your bass, you'll be severely limited in how you can progress on the instrument. It stuns me that people who have been playing the bass for a while will still not have bothered to learn their fretboard inside and out – and then they wonder why they're not progressing as quickly as they think they should. Common sense dictates that we should know the fretboard as thoroughly as possible. It's my job to be as helpful as I can, so let's have a look at some of the ways we can make the process easier.

On the next page you'll find a diagram of the bass neck with all the notes written on it. This is for you to refer to when needed. You'll notice that the diagram goes only as far as the 12th fret. This is because after this fret the notes begin to repeat.

Without further ado, let's examine some of the different ways to get those pesky notes off the fretboard and into your head.

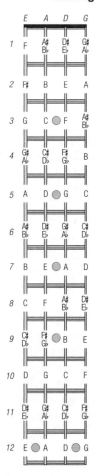

Chart showing note locations along each string

19

Method 1

The first method is to start on the low E string and work your way along it, learning the notes as you go. A basic understanding of the alphabet will help a great deal here, since the same rules apply. If you try to remember that there's a sharp/flat (♯/♭) between each note except for between B and C and between E and F, you should find this method a good place to start. Try to say the notes aloud as you go, as this will help to cement them into your brain. Once you've covered the E string, move on to the other strings.

Method 2

This method is the same as the first in principle, except that it involves learning the notes one fret at a time. Start with the first fret on each string, then the second and so on. You'll find this difficult if you've worked through Method 1, but this highlights a disadvantage of Method 1, which is also shared by Method 2, in that they encourage you to learn the notes parrot-fashion. You'll probably find that you're unable to name any of the notes at random without referring to some of the ones you know before or after them. You might argue that you got there in the end, but you need your knowledge to be more independent. You therefore need to work at randomly naming notes on the neck. Point to any note and name it without having to refer to any others for guidance. Although these two methods have their disadvantages, they're a good place to start.

Method 3

One way that you can expand on the first method and avoid learning by association is to move away from chromatic (one fret at a time) movement. This can be done by starting on the first fret and then ascending to the third, fifth and so on, missing out every other note. The notes you've missed can be played as you descend the string. Try the exercise below and repeat it on the A, D and G strings.

Method 4

This is probably the most musical way to learn your notes and, at the same time, one of the most frustrating. You might already be aware that there is a lot of repetition on the bass neck. Certain notes occur more than once – for example, the open G is the same as the G at the fifth fret D string, the tenth fret A string and the 15th fret E string. Add that to all the other Gs in various octaves and there are a lot of them about.

Starting with the low E, try to play all the Es on your bass, in all the different octaves. Then play all the Fs. This can take a while, so it's probably worth taking it a step at a time, depending on what knowledge of the fretboard you already have. I suggest working on one note at a time and moving on only when you're confident that you know it well.

Many people will find that it's through a combination of these methods that they finally get the notes into their head. It really doesn't matter how you learn them, as long as you learn them. Hopefully you'll find that, once you've learnt them, they stick.

3 NOTATION AND TABLATURE

One of the first questions (or complaints) I hear from students when I bring up the tricky subject of reading music is, 'None of my favourite bass players reads music so why do I need to?' Well, you don't. But even if you don't think you'll ever want or need to read music, it does everyone good to have a basic understanding of the principles involved. It's true that some of the best bass players ever to have walked the Earth don't have a clue how to read music. But equally, there are plenty that can and do read, and it helps them make a living from the thing that they love. Not only will a basic grasp of written music benefit you in every other area of your playing, it will also enable you to communicate with other musicians in a language they'll understand.

Most guitar/bass books available today are notated in a combination of both standard notation and tablature. For those of you who are new to either of these, notation comprises the dots and rhythm parts (the bit we assume is difficult) and tablature is usually written below the notation (the bit that looks not so difficult). All of the music in this book is notated in both ways. We'll talk more about tab in the second half of this chapter, but for now let's have a look at the fundamentals of notation.

Pitch

Music is notated on a set of five horizontal lines called a stave. Notes are placed on the stave either on or between the lines, as shown in the diagram below. At the beginning of the line you'll see what's known as the *bass clef*. A clef is a symbol that tells us what notes the lines and spaces correspond to. For example, the bass clef is occasionally referred to as the *F clef*, as the two dots sit on either side of the line which will hold the note F. From there, it's possible to work out where the rest of the notes will occur. We'll look at those in a moment, but for now here's the bass clef with the open strings of your bass notated on it:

In the next diagram, I've notated all the natural notes from your low E string to the G found at the 12th fret on the G string:

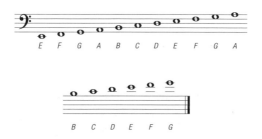

As you can see, sometimes we need to write notes whose pitches are beyond the five lines of the stave. In these instances we have to use *ledger lines*.

Accidentals

You'll notice that so far we haven't covered any sharps or flats – or accidentals, as they're known collectively. That's because these don't occur naturally on the stave; we have to indicate that the note is sharp (♯) or flat (♭) with a special symbol. They look like this in use:

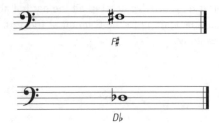

A sharp or flat applies to every occurrence of that note for the rest of the bar. If a following note needs to be made into a natural again, it must be indicated by the natural sign In the next bar, however, the note is automatically natural and you'll need to add another accidental to change it.

As you'll discover, some keys mean that notes will have to be continuously sharpened or flattened. To avoid our music becoming cluttered, we use a system of *key signatures* to indicate that certain notes will be sharp or flat unless indicated otherwise. Key signatures are found at the beginnings of pieces of music and are repeated at the beginning of each new line. Take a look through any music book and you'll see what I mean. In most pieces, you'll see an arrangement of sharps and flats at the start of each line. This tells us what key you're in and which notes are sharp or flat by default. There are 12 keys, each represented by its own key signature:

C Major

F# Major

G Major

D♭ Major

D Major

A♭ Major

A Major

E♭ Major

E Major

B♭ Major

B Major

F Major

Rhythm

Now that we know about staves, notes and accidentals, we can look at how rhythm is notated. Music is divided up into *bars*, or *measures*, by vertical lines known as *bar lines*.

Before we look specifically at rhythms, however, we must look at *time signatures*. A time signature is a device that tells us how rhythms are arranged. Most Western music is written in 4/4 time, which is by far and away the most common time signature and the only one you'll see in this book. The top number tells us how many beats there are in a bar – in this case, four. The lower number tells us the value of those beats, and in this example the value is a quarter-note, also represented by a four. These values will be explained shortly. You can think of a beat as a foot-tap. Try tapping your foot along to a song on the radio – your foot will be marking the beat. You should be able to count one-two-three-four along to your beats. By doing so, you're marking out 4/4 time.

The rhythmic part of notation comes from the stems and their various groupings that lead upwards or downwards from the notes. There are several different rhythmic values we can assign to a note – for example, we can make a note last for one beat, two beats, half a beat, a quarter of a beat and so on. The chart on the next page shows the different rhythmic values available and their corresponding rests. You'll notice that I have included both English and American terminology, but I prefer to use the American – it certainly makes more sense!

By using combinations of these rhythms, we can notate how we want our music to sound.

In the examples that follow, I will illustrate some of these rhythms. The second part of each example illustrates the use of the rest for the rhythm in question.

In the first example, there are four quarter notes in a bar – that's one for each beat (or foot-tap):

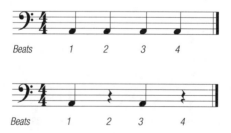

29

basic Bass Workout

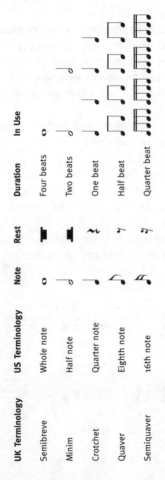

UK Terminology	US Terminology	Note	Rest	Duration	In Use
Semibreve	Whole note			Four beats	
Minim	Half note			Two beats	
Crotchet	Quarter note			One beat	
Quaver	Eighth note			Half beat	
Semiquaver	16th note			Quarter beat	

Next is a bar of half notes. These last for two beats each, so there will be two of them in a bar:

The next example is a bar of eighth notes. Two eighth notes comprise a single beat, so we can play eight of these in a bar:

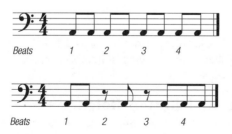

You'll also notice that, where possible, our eighth notes have been *beamed* together in groups of two. This is for ease of reading, as it makes it clearer for us to see the beat divisions.

Next is a bar of 16th notes. As illustrated in the table earlier, there are four 16th notes per beat, so we can have 16 16th notes in a bar.

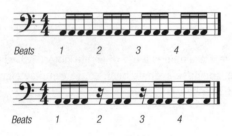

Obviously, in order to cover the many different rhythmic possibilities, we are going to have to mix and match our rhythms.

Tied And Dotted Notes

That's all very well, but what if we want a note to last for a beat and a half? Or for three quarters of a beat?

We can use ties or dots to notate those variations. A tie tells you to you hold a note for its duration and the duration of the note that it's tied to.

For example, if you wanted a note to last for a beat and a half, you could write this:

Beats   1   2   3   4

We could also notate the same thing with a dotted note. Adding a dot after a note extends its value by 50 per cent, so a dotted quarter note lasts for a quarter note plus an eighth note, or a beat and a half:

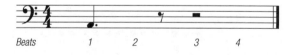

Beats   1   2   3   4

Dotted notes are particularly useful for dividing up 16th-note rhythms, as shown in the illustration at the top of the next page:

Triplets

The last rhythm to look at is the triplet. A triplet is three evenly played notes in the space of two. There is not a mathematically correct way of notating triplets with the rhythms we have examined so far, so they must be written slightly differently.

In the example below, I've written out a bar of eighth-note triplets:

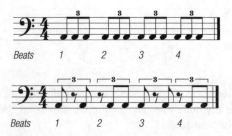

You'll notice the numeral 3 over the groupings – this is necessary to indicate a triplet.

We can also play quarter-note triplets. Again, the number 3 must be added over the grouping to indicate three notes in the space of two:

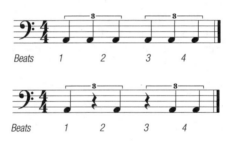

Tablature

Tablature, or *tab*, as it's commonly known, is often frowned upon by the 'serious' bass-playing community for being simplistic and having little musical content. It's true that you can get only so much from reading tab, since it doesn't contain any rhythmic information, leaving you having to either guess how to play the notes or listen closely to the track. But tab has its advantages, too. It's great for beginners and works well

basic Bass Workout

as a quick-start method for learning your favourite songs. It also shows you where to play the notes on the bass, whereas notation leaves that decision to your best judgement.

Tab is notated on a stave, which is read from left to right, much like standard notation. However, instead of a stave with five lines, tab uses a four-line stave with each line representing one of the strings on your bass. The top line is the G string, the bottom one the E string and the middle two the A and D strings respectively.

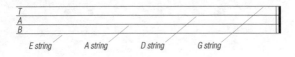

E string   A string   D string   G string

Notes are notated according to the fret they occur on. The B found at the seventh fret on the E string would be notated thus:

A G major scale would be written like this:

Any notes played together, such as chords and double stops, would be notated like this:

```
T ————— 13 ——————————————————————————
A ————— 12 ——————————————————————————
B ————— 0  ——————————————————————————
```

That's about as far as tab-reading goes, but it's lot easier on the eye than standard notation, I think you'll agree!

Remember to bear in mind that tab doesn't give you all the information you need. As I mentioned at the beginning of this section, there's absolutely no rhythmic information contained in tab, so the format does have its limits. However, if you've never read music of any kind, it's the perfect place to start.

4 PRACTISING

For some people, the very thought of practising – even the mention of the word – is enough to send shivers down their spines. But the fact remains that, if you want to be better at something, you need to practise. However, while many bassists think of practice as being pointless hours spent in front of the metronome playing through endless scales and arpeggios, it can actually be very different.

Firstly, you don't need to spend five hours a day practising in order to notice an improvement in your playing. In fact, I can assure you that half an hour a day, every day, will yield very surprising results. Secondly, it doesn't have to be boring – honestly! You could even learn to love it.

Students often ask me how often they should practise. The answer depends on what you want to get out of your instrument – as I said earlier, you get out only what you put in. It stands to reason that, if all you want to do is learn rock songs and play in pubs, you won't require as much practice as the guy who wants to set the world on fire with his mastery of jazz soloing. However, I believe that every bass player should practise every day. As I said, I know for a fact that half an hour a day will change your playing.

Making A Practice Schedule

What you practise depends on what you want to do with your instrument. Once you know this, you'll know what to focus on and set your goals accordingly. Goals are important for all musicians, as they give you direction and, when attained, add extra momentum to your enthusiasm. I find that a well-thought-out practice schedule helps me to achieve what I want out of my playing. Here are some of the topics that I might practise.

- **Warm-ups** – These are essential for every bass player. It can be very damaging to your hands to play the bass without properly warming up. Warming up can consist of playing chromatic patterns, a series of scales or just some simple lines at a comfortable tempo. I would recommend doing a minimum of five to ten minutes of warming up before playing.

- **Scale Knowledge** – This is important to any bass player who wants freedom on their instrument.

Scales can also replace pattern exercises as more musical warm-ups.

- **Sight-Reading** – This is one section that really does depend on what you want from your instrument. For the most part, only bassists who consider playing for a living will feel that they need this skill. Nevertheless, I consider it very important.

- **Technique** – Having problems with your slap technique? Your string crossing or your raking? Practice will cure all of this, and it's important to devote time to honing your technique.

- **Tunes** – The more songs you know, the easier you'll find life as a bass player. Whether it's learning the new song by your favourite band or finding your way through a tricky jazz chart, this is one of the most important aspects of practice.

- **Difficult Licks** – I also find it useful to keep a small list of licks that I struggle with. A little work on them every day ensures that I progress with them.

Learning It Twice

Have you ever tried learning something new only to find that your hands can't keep up with your brain or vice versa? I have, and I've come to the conclusion that you need to learn new material twice: first in your head and then in your hands.

When approaching a new lick try this: look through the music first without touching your bass. Check out notes and position shifts, anything that may present a problem. Now grab your bass and play through it slowly. Give your fingers a chance to learn where they need to go. Go over tricky passages bit by bit, making sure that you understand what's going on before progressing too far.

Now work with your new music and practise it. Play it a little quicker if you can. Build on what you've learnt so far, concentrating on the weaker aspects and bringing them up to speed. This approach is infinitely better than rushing in and trying to play an awkward piece at speed straight away.

Your Surroundings

You need to be comfortable when you practise. By 'comfortable' I mean sat in a chair that supports your back and in quiet, pleasant surroundings. Finding a good chair to sit in is important, as playing the bass tends to encourage us to hunch. Find a chair that supports your lower back and resist the temptation to hunch over, staring at the fretboard. Don't practise sat in bed, on the sofa or on the floor!

It's important to try to find a time in the day when you're least likely to be disturbed – you're not going to get anything constructive done with people walking in and out of the room and talking to you, so try to find a quiet practice area. I also find it very useful to be organised. Have everything you need with you: music paper, books, pens, leads and so on should all be within easy reach.

Metronome Practice

Practising with either a metronome or a drum machine is essential. I was once taught a very useful practising trick with a metronome. Set your tempo, but imagine that the click is the offbeat. Your tempo will look like this:

    one (click) two (click) three (click) four (click)...

The benefit of this system is that, because you're not actually playing on the click, it checks you after you've played. Learning to work with a metronome encourages good time-keeping.

Even if you're still not particularly enamoured with practising, you will notice that, aside from the obvious benefit of improving on the bass, it will help your creativity. As part of my practice regime, I play grooves along with a beat. I try to alternate my rhythms so that one day I'm playing funk, whereas another day I might be playing reggae, and so on. Mostly I'll come up with either a line, a fill or a chord that interests me, and that I probably would never have thought of ordinarily.

Now, here's the key to this: if you come with a new idea, write it down, or record it if you have the capability. I keep a note pad handy and jot down everything – solo ideas, chord voicings, fills, the lot. This means that I have a note pad full of ideas that I can continue practising, add to my repertoire or develop as I see fit. For me, practising aids creativity, which helps me enjoy it a whole lot more.

5 MAJOR SCALES

Welcome to the first of two chapters on everyone's least-favourite subject: scales. Now, I'm not going to try to convince you that scales are particularly enjoyable to play, because they're not, but if you want to develop your bass playing, you're going to need them, and what's more, you're going to have to practise them. I'm hoping that when you know just a little more about them – and you begin to see how they are going to help you become a better player and maybe it will make all that practice a little easier to bear.

Scales are the raw material of music – the bricks we build our musical houses out of, if you like. For a bass player, and indeed any musician, scales serve many useful purposes, and you'll benefit from having at least some knowledge of them.

I'm often asked, what are scales actually for? There are several answers: they will help free your creativity on the bass and enable you to play in all keys; they will enable you to solo convincingly; they make good warm-up exercises; they're great for left- and right-hand development and dexterity. I could go on, but suffice to say they're basically pretty useful.

As I've already mentioned, to get the most out of scales you'll need to practise them quite religiously. I strongly recommend working them into your daily practice routine. Ten to fifteen minutes a day working methodically with your scales will improve your playing in many directions at once.

There are two main types of scale: major and minor. What follows is a fairly in-depth look at major scales and what I think is the best way to go about learning them. Fear not, I will attempt to take you through them a step at a time, demystifying them and explaining carefully as I go.

The information presented here is designed to be cumulative – by working through this chapter in order you'll be gradually adding to your knowledge in small chunks, and by the end you should be well equipped to start on Chapter 6, 'Minor Scales' . I strongly recommend that you take this information at a pace you're comfortable with and learn it thoroughly.

With the following exercises, I'm going to assume that you know the fretboard of your bass pretty well – you won't be able to find your way around these scales properly without knowing where all the notes are. As discussed in Chapter 2, good fretboard knowledge is fundamental to any bass player, so if you have any doubt about what some of those frets are for, I suggest that you do a little homework! It's also worth mentioning that you should familiarise yourself with the sound of the major scale – it should be familiar to you; it's basically the same as that old tune 'Doh-Ray-Me'. Keep your ears open when you're playing, don't shut off and don't just play through them mindlessly – listen to what you're doing.

It's also useful to try singing the scale as you play it. Don't be shy! It's very useful for a bass player to develop his/her ear, and singing along helps!

Let's start at the very beginning and look at how to play a basic major scale. Here's the fingering for a C major scale starting from the C at the third fret on the A string:

Exercise 1

In between the staves I've written the left-hand fingering that I would suggest using. This system is known as the 'finger per fret' system and is explained in more detail in Chapter 7. It's fairly obvious when you look at what we are playing. A major scale in this position covers four frets and we have four fingers on our left hand – makes sense to use them all, doesn't it? This is illustrated below:

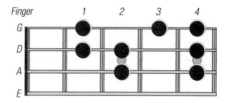

Using this system will greatly help the dexterity of your left hand and encourage you to use all of your fingers.

It stands to reason that, by moving this shape around, you could play a major scale in any key you liked simply by moving the whole thing to a different fret. Go ahead and try it: move this pattern up so that your second finger is on the eighth fret, an F. Because the intervals

basic Bass Workout

(ie the distances between the notes) haven't changed, the sound is almost the same; you're simply playing it in a new key.

I'm a great advocate of playing through all of your major scales at least a couple of times a week. It doesn't take long and is good for your hands, your ears and definitely for your brain. I practise my scales according to a sequence called the *circle of fifths*. This is simply a representation of all 12 keys, each one a fifth up from the last.

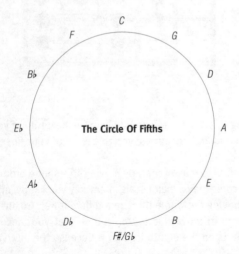

Set a metronome going at a nice easy tempo –
somewhere around 80 beats per minute (bpm) – and
play though your C major scale.

Next, move on to the G major scale, then the D, and
so on, as shown in the illustration over the page. Try
not to break your flow between scales – you have time
to be thinking ahead and looking to where you'll need
to move as you play. The first three keys – C, G, and D
– are shown overleaf.

Make sure that you can play and understand what we've
covered so far before moving on. At this point you don't
need to know what notes are in each scale and why –
we'll get to that shortly. This exercise should serve to
get you comfortable playing the major scale in different
places on the bass, and it also makes a good warm-
up exercise!

Content Over Patterns

You'd be forgiven for thinking that the obvious thing
to do next would be to steam ahead and learn two-
octave major scales. Well, here's a surprise: that's not
what we're going to do – at least not yet. I believe
that doing this would result in simply learning another
pattern and not addressing the notes themselves –
not learning much actual content. Instead, I'm going

Exercise 2

to suggest what I believe is a much more musical path. You might have to work a little harder, but I think you'll find that the benefits are significantly greater than they would be if I simply gave you some patterns and showed you how to shift them around.

No, I believe the best way forward is to go back now and learn the notes involved in a one-octave scale and then apply that knowledge to playing two octave scales and more.

Let's go back to that C major scale we started with. You'll notice that it's made up purely of natural notes – no sharps or flats involved. In fact, it's the only major scale that has no accidentals, which makes it the perfect place to start. Here are the notes of the C major scale:

C D E F G A B C

Armed with this knowledge, it stands to reason that we could pick any C on the bass and play the scale from there. Start on the same C as before and play through all the natural notes on the same string until you get to C again. If you did it correctly, you'll have played this:

Exercise 3

basic Bass Workout

By knowing the content of the scale rather than just a pattern, which is of limited real use, we can put our knowledge to work in new ways. If I'm doing my job properly here, playing a two-octave major scale shouldn't sound quite so bad now...

Let's give it a try. Start on the C and then play up through the natural notes to the next C, then to the next one. You'll undoubtedly notice that at some point you're going to have to move to another string. But where? There are many points at which you could jump, and no right or wrong ones. The benefit of what you've just learned is that, by knowing the notes in the scale, you can play through it in many ways – a different way each time, if you wish. This helps you to learn the scale over the whole fretboard and is the benefit of learning scales as content rather than learning them as patterns.

Exercise 4a

I did promise to be helpful, however, so here's another way that you could have played your two-octave C major scale:

Exercise 4b

If this is all new to you, then I would suggest you take it all nice and slow and just practise a little every day. For the first few days, you'll probably find yourself sticking to the fingerings I suggested above, but I'm betting that after a while you'll start to notice different ones, too.

The Next Step

Once you're completely happy with your first scale, it's time to learn another one. Don't forget that there are 12 keys to learn! Fortunately, if you learn all of your scales in the order shown by the circle of fifths, you'll be building on what you've learnt previously, and in small, manageable steps.

Consulting the circle of fifths will reveal that the next scale is G major. To start with, let's play a one-octave

basic Bass Workout

G major scale starting on the G located at the third fret on the E string.

Assuming that you know the fretboard, you'll have noticed that this scale differs very little (by only one note) to the C major scale. In fact, you should notice that it's almost identical. This is because, by moving sequentially around the circle of fifths in this manner, each scale will contain only one different note from the last. Cool, huh? If you don't believe me, take a pen and paper and write the notes down for yourself. You'll see this:

G   A   B   C   D   E   F♯   G

The G major scale is different from the C major by just one note – our F has become an F♯.

Now try playing through a G major scale on just the E string, armed with this new knowledge. The illustration below shows what you'll have hopefully ended up playing:

Now let's try a two-octave G major scale. As with the C major scale, there are many different ways of playing this and you should avoid sticking to any particular one. Good fretboard knowledge will enable you to find many different possibilities. Below I've illustrated a couple of ways in which you can do it:

basic Bass Workout

There are ten more major scales for you to learn. Be careful not to bite off more than you can chew and move on to the next scale only when you're happy with the last one. Learning your scales in this way is much more musical and really tests your knowledge of the fretboard. With scales, as with any other aspect of playing the bass, if you find it difficult I would suggest that you try to see it as a challenge rather than an obstacle and push past it. If you find something difficult, that usually means that it's worth doing!

6 MINOR SCALES

Unfortunately, minor scales are slightly more complicated than their major cousins. This is mainly because there are no less than three different types of minor scale. These three types are the *natural minor*, the *harmonic minor* and the *melodic minor*. Now for some good news: straight away we are going to dispense with one of these, the melodic minor, as it's not a scale with which you as a bassist need to be immediately familiar. Here's another piece of good news: if you have successfully worked through the previous chapter on major scales, you're going to find this chapter pretty easy, since we're going to be building on what knowledge of scales you've already acquired – all will become clear soon, I promise.

The Natural Minor Scale

We're going to start with the natural minor scale. Now, as I mentioned above, if you've worked through the previous chapter on major scales, you won't find these too hard. 'Why's that?' I hear you ask. The answer is that you already know them. Suspend your disbelief for a moment so that I can attempt to explain: every natural minor scale is, in fact, one of the major scales you've learnt already, just starting from a different note – in musical terms, we say that they are related. Consider the following fretboard diagram of a natural minor scale:

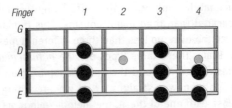

Let's play through this scale from the A on your E string, as in Exercise 1 below. You'll immediately hear that our A minor scale doesn't sound quite as jolly as the good old major scale. In fact, at a very basic level you can think of major scales as sounding 'happy' and minor ones as 'sad'.

Exercise 1

Now let's examine the notes you've just played. If you write down each note in the A minor scale, you'll get this: A, B, C, D, E, F, G, A.

I'm hoping that alarm bells are now ringing in your head and that you have spotted that this scale doesn't contain any sharps or flats. This being the case, you might also have noticed that it contains the same notes as the C major scale – but they're now in a different order. This is because the A minor scale is the *relative minor* of the C major scale.

Relative Minors

Each major scale has a relative minor scale which contains exactly the same notes. To find a major scale's corresponding relative minor scale, you simply count up through the degrees of the major scale to the sixth degree – the relative minor scale is built on the sixth degree of the major scale.

$$C \quad D \quad E \quad F \quad G \quad \widehat{A} \quad B \quad C$$
$$1 \quad 2 \quad 3 \quad 4 \quad 5 \quad \widehat{6} \quad 7 \quad 8$$

This is true of every major scale, so you'll now be able to go through each of your major scales and find their relative minors. Here, though, I've done it for you:

basic Bass Workout

Major Scale	Relative Minor Scale
C	Am
G	Em
D	Bm
A	F#m
E	C#m
B	G#m
F#/Gb	D#/Ebm
Db	Bbm
Ab	Fm
Eb	Cm
Bb	Gm
F	Dm

As I mentioned in the previous chapter, it's important to learn the content of the scale rather than simply learn a load of patterns, so for the rest of the exercises I'm going to make the following two, rather bold, assumptions:

• That you know your fretboard;
• That you know the note content of at least some, if not all, of your major scales.

With these assumptions in mind, let's think about how we might play an A minor scale on just one string. As I stated above, if you know your fretboard, this won't present a problem to you. A quick recap on what we've covered so far in this chapter will tell you that A minor is related to C major and therefore contains the same notes – no sharps or flats. Common sense dictates that playing an A minor scale from A will include only the natural notes. So without further ado, let's give it a try:

Exercise 2

Hopefully you've played the same as the exercise above.

Now, by combining our knowledge of the scale with our knowledge of the fretboard, we should be able to play a two-octave A minor scale. As in the previous chapter, there are numerous different fingerings for doing this, and the following exercise is just one of them:

Exercise 3

basic Bass Workout

Here's another way you could have played it, this time starting from the open A string:

Exercise 4

As with the major scales, you should explore the different ways of playing this scale. To begin with you may find that you stick to the two patterns I've illustrated here, which is fine, but as you become familiar with the sound and notes of the scale you're bound to find new ways to play it. Try to cover as much of the instrument as you can when learning a scale – scales are most useful when you can play them anywhere on the instrument.

If you find an area of the bass you're not confident with – the higher register, for example – make a point of learning what notes live up there and practising your scales there as well.

At this point I suggest that you make sure you've fully understood the concepts presented thus far. If you find yourself struggling with these exercises I would suggest that you stop here and spend some time working on your fretboard knowledge and what we've looked at so far in this chapter.

The next step is to start learning the other minor scales. If you know your major scales, this should be fairly straightforward since you will in effect be playing exactly the same notes as the corresponding relative major. Try to memorise which major and minor scales relate to each other – it will make things easier. I recommend consulting the chart shown earlier in this chapter and working through it methodically – A minor, E minor, and so on. Be sure to take the rest of the minor scales one at a time and be careful not to bite off more than you can chew. For reference, here's the next scale in the sequence, E minor, shown here in a two-octave version:

Exercise 5

Looking at the scale and the chart will reveal that the
E minor scale is related to the G major scale and
therefore contains the same notes – all naturals except
the F, which has become an F#:

E F# G A B C D E

Harmonic Minor Scales

Before you start on harmonic minor scales, I strongly
recommend that you have a good understanding of
what we've covered so far on natural minors. By doing
so you'll save yourself a lot of work, since you're going
to build on your knowledge of the natural minors.

Harmonic minor scales differ from natural minor scales
by just one note, the seventh degree of the scale, or the
leading note, as it's known. In the harmonic minor scale
the seventh is sharpened – so, in the example of the A
minor scale, the G is sharpened, becoming a G#. Here's
the fingerboard pattern for an A harmonic minor scale:

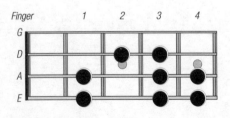

Play through the scale shown below. You'll immediately hear that it has a distinctly different sound to the natural minor scale. It's obviously still a minor scale, but it has a more 'Spanish' flavour to it, for want of a better word!

Exercise 6

By knowing the theory behind this scale – that it's the same as the natural minor but with a sharpened leading note – we should be able to adapt our natural minors to harmonic minors by simply altering that one note. Let's put that theory into practice and play an A harmonic minor scale on just the E string:

Exercise 7

basic Bass Workout

Again, using what we've learned so far, we can adapt a two-octave A natural minor scale into an A minor harmonic scale:

Exercise 8

Here's an alternative fingering:

Exercise 9

You'll notice that the interval between the F and G♯ presents some fingering problems in that it's a larger interval than you would expect to find in a major or minor scale. Make sure that, when playing through any of the previous three exercises, you follow the fingering that I have notated between the staves.

There's little else I need to say about harmonic minors at this point. Now it's simply down to you to learn the other 11!

There's a lot of information contained in these chapters. It's vital that you take these exercises at a pace that you can deal with and not feel obligated to move through them too quickly. Good luck with them, and trust me – you'll be glad you made the effort!

7 THE LEFT HAND

Many people neglect their left hands, not realising that they need just as much attention as their right. Every player has four fingers on their left hand, but many don't utilise the full potential of them. It's all too common for bassists to neglect the third or fourth fingers, whereas if they were to put them to use they would find many bass lines and chord shapes a lot easier. Being able to play fast and, more importantly, accurately doesn't just involve the right hand; you will need to develop your left hand as well and strengthen up those weaker fingers. That's what this chapter is all about.

Fretboard Accuracy

Firstly, you need to make sure that you're playing on the correct part of the fret. You'd be forgiven for thinking that, because your bass has frets, you can play anywhere between the frets and it will sound okay. Technically that's true, but by ignoring accurate placement you will create problems in your playing that will be trickier to solve later on.

Try playing a G on your E string with your finger in the centre of the fret. You should find it sounds pretty good. Now move your finger closer to either one of the frets. You'll hear that you're starting to get some nasty fret buzz. We want to keep noises like that out of our bass playing, so for all of these exercises and, indeed, for everything you play, try to keep to the centre of the fret.

Chromatic Exercises

You may have seen some of the following exercises before and are now groaning, and I guess they are pretty boring, but while they might sound bad and have little actual musical content, they do serve one useful purpose, and that is to get your fingers working in all sorts of unusual ways. In each of these exercises, we'll utilise the finger-per-fret method. Each exercise is based on four chromatic frets (that's four frets next to each other), and since we have four fingers on our left hands it makes sense to use them all. As the exercises have little musical relevance, I've notated them in tab only. All of these exercises are to be played slowly – accuracy and tone are the important points here and there's little to be gained from playing them too quickly.

In Exercise 1 we're going to use the first four frets on each string in ascending, then descending, order. Remember to keep each finger in the centre of the fret:

basic Bass Workout

```
T|                    |                    |   1—2 -3 - 4    | 1 - 2 - 3 - 4 |
A|                    | 1 - 2 - 3 - 4      |                 |               |
B| 1 - 2 - 3 - 4      |                    |                 |               |
```

```
T| 4 - 3 - 2 - 1      |                    |                 |               |
A|                    | 4 - 3 - 2 - 1      |                 |               |
B|                    |                    | 4 — 3 - 2 — 1   | 4 - 3 - 2 - 1 |
```

Exercise 1

When ascending, try to keep each finger in place while you play the next. If you have small hands, or find that they aren't sufficiently flexible to stretch like this, try moving the exercise to a higher fret where the spacing is narrower – the fifth fret is a good place. When you become happy in this position, see if you can move back to the first fret.

The next exercise is basically the same, except that we're going to apply a new rule: when you run out of fingers, move up one fret. Confused? Me too, but a quick look at the tab should clear things up:

Exercise 2

This next exercise goes by many different names, but I like to call it the Snake.

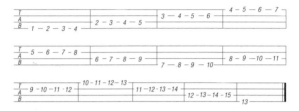

Exercise 3

So far, we've used our fingers only in ascending and descending order: 1, 2, 3, 4 and 4, 3, 2, 1. There are hundreds of different combinations of patterns for your fingers to explore and I'll leave it up to you to discover all of the various possibilities.

For now, let's look at three different fingerings, each one using a different finger to lead with. This exercise is fingered 3, 4, 2, 1:

Exercise 4

basic Bass Workout

Now let's try 2, 1, 3, 4:

Exercise 5

And finally 1, 4, 3, 2:

```
T
A
B  1 - 4 - 3 - 2    1 - 4 - 3 - 2    1 — 4 — 3 — 2    1 — 4 — 3 — 2
```

Exercise 6

As I said, there are many different combinations and I'm sure that you'll be able to work out plenty more for yourself. If you find one that's particularly difficult, add it immediately to your practice routine. If you can't do it, you need to practise it, since whatever fingers are holding you back are clearly too weak and need strengthening.

8 PHRASING TECHNIQUES

Now that you've looked at the various ways in which you can strengthen and develop your left-hand fingers, it's time to look at the some of the phrasing techniques available. The left hand is very important for phrasing, which forms a large part of that indefinable character which gives each player his own unique sound. The way in which you phrase something defines who you are as a player, and the more phrasing choices you have, the smoother and more fluid your playing will be.

The left hand is responsible for a whole host of phrasing techniques, from slurs (hammer-ons and pull-offs) to string bending and all the different varieties of vibrato. The good thing about all of the phrasing tools that we will look at over the next few pages is that they can be applied to any style of music. Once you've mastered them, you'll use them every day in your playing – in fact, it's pretty likely that you already do. In this chapter we will examine each technique in turn.

Slurs: Hammer-ons And Pull-offs

These two strange-sounding customers are types of slurs. A slur is defined as 'a curved line written over two notes indicating that they are to be played legato or in the same stroke'. Here's an example of both a hammer-on and a pull-off, both of which are described in detail below.

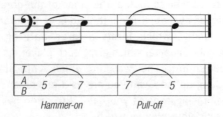

Hammer-on   Pull-off

The Hammer-on

This is the first and most obvious phrasing tool, and it's also one of the most useful. With a hammer-on, a note is played and then another left-hand finger 'hammers' on another note further up on the same string. Using this technique you can play two or more notes after plucking the string only once.

Let's try the example above. Play the D at the fifth fret of your A string – use the first finger of your left hand to fret the note. Once you've played the note, bring your third or fourth finger of the left hand down onto the E at the seventh fret. You'll need to do this quite firmly in order to produce a strong, clear note, and you should aim for both notes to be pretty much the same volume.

The Pull-off

The pull-off is basically a backwards hammer-on. To play a pull-off, place your left-hand first finger on the D at the fifth fret of the A string. Place the third or fourth finger on the E at the seventh fret. Play the string – this will sound the note E. As the note is still ringing, remove your fourth finger from the string. This will allow the fretted D to sound. You will find that you need to pull at the string with your finger slightly as you lift it – this will create movement in the string and allow the note to sound. Again, try to aim for the same volume with both notes.

While it's important to try to play both notes of each example at the same volume, you'll also notice a difference in attack. The first one will have a slightly sharper attack because it has been plucked, while the second will sound different because you've slurred it. Hammer-ons and pull-offs enable you to play in a more fluid, legato manner, which can only be a good thing. Let's take a look at some of the other slurring options.

Trills

A trill is a combination of hammer-ons and pull-offs played in rapid succession. As in the other examples, only the first note is struck; the rest of the notes are created by hammering on and pulling off. A trill is indicated by the letters *tr* over a note, followed by a wavy line. A trill lasts for the duration of the note over which it's written.

Vibrato

Vibrato is a rapid variation in the pitch of a note, played by shaking the fretting finger vertically or horizontally. Vibrato is notated by a wavy line over the note. The method of vibrato most commonly used by guitarists and bassists is to shake the string vertically. To do this, play a note, then move the string up and down slightly with your left-hand finger – you'll hear the note 'wobble'.

The other way to play vibrato is to shake your finger from side to side on the string. This method derives from the world of classical music and is used by violinists and other members of the string section. It's particularly effective on a fretless bass.

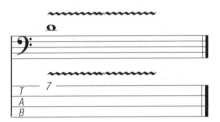

String Bending

String bending is very popular with guitarists and bassists, and it's one of the most expressive phrasing tools you have available. Bending the string can be used in place of a hammer-on to raise the pitch of a note. It can be also be used as a slurring tool.

Take a look at the notation for string bending that appears at the top of the next page. In the first example you can see how the hammer-on I have illustrated could

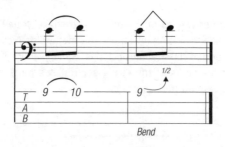

Bend

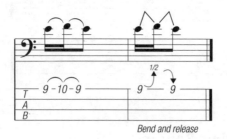

Bend and release

be played as a string bend. In the second example you can see the hammer-on/pull-off figure played as a bend and release.

Notice how string bends are notated – bending a note up a to the pitch of the fret above it requires an upward-sweeping arrow with a 1/2 above it. The 1/2 refers to half a tone – or a semitone, in technical terms. If we wanted to bend the note up a tone – to the pitch of the note two frets up – we would write 'full' instead of '1/2'. A bend and release is notated in the same way as a bend, but with a second downward-sweeping arrow to indicate the release.

I recommend learning to use each of the techniques described in this chapter. Not only will they enable you to play in a smoother and more graceful way but they will also help you to define your own voice on the bass.

9 FINGERSTYLE

Fingerstyle playing is probably the most commonly used method to play the bass and is a technique favoured by many of the greatest players. While it may not offer the immense speed that plectrum playing allows, it more than makes up for this with its many other advantages. With fingerstyle playing comes greater versatility, particularly with regard to string crossing and muting. You'll also find that it gives you more options, tone-wise.

In this chapter I'm going to take you through the various aspects of fingerstyle playing that I believe will either get you started or help you to improve on what you already have.

Hand Position

The first thing to consider is your hand position. Most basses have one or two pick-ups located on the body and these serve another purpose besides amplifying your playing efforts – they make a good place to anchor your thumb! It is very important to have your thumb anchored to the bass in some way when playing fingerstyle as you need a solid location to play from. (Try playing with your thumb floating in mid-air – it's much harder!) By experimenting with your hand position, you should find that the tone you get out of the bass changes in relation to where you pluck the strings. Playing back by the bridge and anchoring your thumb on the back pick-up (if you have one) will give you a harder, more precise-sounding tone that's great for funk lines and for playing quicker patterns. The tone towards the neck end of the bass is fuller and rounder but with less bite. Most players will alter their hand positions slightly depending on what style they are playing.

Plucking The Strings

The next thing to consider is how you pluck the strings. You should aim to play the strings with your fingertips. This may cause some discomfort to begin with, especially if you're new to the instrument. It's possible that you'll develop some mild blisters if you overdo it, so take it slow and don't get too carried away just yet. Eventually the ends of your fingers will develop calluses.

It's very important to minimise the amount of movement in your fingers as you play. Try to move the finger from the second knuckle rather than the first. As with any technique, economy of motion is very important and less movement means smoother playing.

You'll also need to work on alternating your fingers in the pattern that suits you – 1, 2, 1, 2 or 2, 1, 2, 1, depending on which finger you feel most comfortable leading with.

For Exercise 1 you're just going to play eighth notes on the E string. Keep an eye on your fingers and make sure that you're alternating them properly – most beginners find that they're focusing so much on their left-hand technique that they don't realise that they're favouring one right-hand finger over another. Playing a simple pattern such as this should enable you to be looking at your plucking hand:

Exercise 1

You'll notice that I've indicated right-hand fingering

between the staves. I've written in these numbers with the assumption in mind that you're leading with your first finger. If you're leading with your second, simply swap the numbers. It doesn't matter which you use, providing that you're alternating continually.

Exercise 2 continues in the same style, but now we move on to the A string as well:

Exercise 2

Moving to another string may present some problems for you. You may find that, when you pluck the A string, your finger is also striking the E string lightly as it comes off the A, creating a open-string hum in the background. You need to avoid extraneous noise like this at all times and keep your playing as neat as possible. Thankfully, there is a solution, one which I rather affectionately refer to as the 'Travelling Thumb'…

The Travelling Thumb

You'll recall at the beginning of this chapter that I talked about the importance of anchoring your thumb on the pick-up for stability. Don't worry, I'm not about to go back on what I've already told you – this remains an important aspect of fingerstyle playing – we're just going to make some modifications. When you play the E string of your bass as in Exercise 1, there's no way for you to be touching the other strings with your right hand and creating excess noise. However, when you play any of the other strings – A, D or G – you have plenty of scope for doing so. To get around this, you can move your thumb anchor according to what string you're playing. For example, if you were playing on the A string, your thumb would move from the pick-up onto the E string, muting it. This technique works for the other strings as well. As you move across the strings, try to keep your thumb anchored on the string above. This is the Travelling Thumb, and it will help to keep excess noise out of your playing.

Exercise 3 uses all four strings. As you work through the exercise, keep in mind your thumb position and be sure to move it accordingly. You should also avoid any pauses that might occur as you move your hand from string to string:

Exercise 3

This will get trickier with the more string-crossing you have to do. So far you've only jumped from string to adjacent string, but often you'll have to jump or 'skip' over a string – to play an octave, for example. In the next example, you will have to jump from playing notes on the E string to playing the D string. Be sure your thumb travels with you!

Exercise 4

This might feel awkward to begin with but it's a technique worth persevering with. It's much easier to learn this early on in your playing than it is to discover you need it later on and have to go back and retrain your hands. Trust me, I'm trying to get you into good habits here, in some cases by avoiding my bad ones! Try to incorporate this technique into the other aspects of your practice schedule – the perfect place to use it, for example, is when playing scales.

Raking

You might find it uncomfortable to alternate your fingers and cross strings at the same time. Sometimes, when playing from higher strings to lower ones it can be easier to use a rake. I don't mean the commonly used garden tool, rather a technique whereby the finger that has just played the string can 'rake' back to the string below and play that string too. You can try this by playing a note on your G string and allowing your finger to come to rest on the D string. You can then play a note on the D string with the same finger. Doing this can help to smoothe out your technique even further.

Play through a descending C major scale using this technique. I've indicated a rake with an *r* before the finger number:

Exercise 5

More Right-Hand Muting

You might be wondering what happens if you're playing a fast passage that crosses strings frequently – it's obviously not practical for your right-hand thumb to keep jumping from one string to another. In a case such as this, I would simply anchor the right-hand thumb on the pick-up and leave it there. I would use a combination of left- and right-hand muting in this example to keep it neat. Next we'll look at another way in which we can mute with the right hand.

In all of the examples so far, the notes have been allowed to ring for their entire duration – you haven't yet played any short, staccato notes. As with all techniques, there are a number of ways to shorten and mute notes, some of which are more successful than others. So what do we do when we want those funky, staccato 16th-note grooves? The answer lies in your right-hand technique.

basic Bass Workout

Try this exercise: play through Exercise 1 in this chapter again and look closely at your right-hand fingers as you play. Play the string with your first or second finger and then alternate so the next finger plays the next note. There is no rest – as each finger touches the string, it's playing it, and the string sounds until you play the next note. Playing in this way enables you to produce long, sustained notes and smooth bass parts.

Now, to make these notes shorter, more staccato, you could apply some left-hand muting by lifting the fretting fingers off the fretboard slightly. However, it would be very difficult to play a complex bass part in this way. A simpler method is to use the right-hand fingers. Try this: as you play a note, immediately bring your next finger into position and allow it to rest on the string ready to play the next note. By doing so, you'll stop the string from ringing, shortening the note. Each finger can therefore serve two purposes: playing the string and stopping it. You'll find this to be a very useful muting tool.

Let's take a look at it in the context of an exercise. In this example I'm going to play through the same bass part twice, once with no right-hand muting and once with the muting, producing clipped staccato notes:

Exercise 6

Ghost Notes And 16th-Note Lines

Ghost notes are short, percussive notes that give a fingerstyle line a stronger sense of groove. They're used to great effect by players such as Rocco Prestia, Flea and the late James Jamerson. It doesn't matter what style you're playing in, be it funk, reggae or blues, ghost notes add character and feel to a line. To play a ghost note, let your fretting fingers up from the fretboard slightly. Doing so will prevent the note from ringing properly so that, when you strike the string, you hear a percussive note. In the following example, play a group of notes as you normally would, then a group of ghost notes so that you can hear the difference.

Exercise 7

Now let's incorporate some ghost notes into a groove. You should hear what a difference they make:

Exercise 8

Those ghost notes certainly add an extra funky and percussive element, I'm sure you'll agree. You'll also notice how I made use of 16th notes in this bass part.

Lines like this are tricky to execute flawlessly and require a thorough understanding of all of the concepts presented in this chapter. While it should be your goal to play accurately rather than fast, I must admit that lines like this are fun to play and, if played accurately, can groove really well within the right type of song. Let's take a look at how to develop 16th-note lines such as these.

This exercise should help you to get started. You'll need to work on playing 16th notes with a metronome at a slow tempo in addition to working on all of the concepts presented in this chapter. Start the exercise at around 80 beats per minute and move on only when you feel completely comfortable with the tempo.

Exercise 9

Don't be tempted to go too fast too soon, and remember to alternate your picking fingers continually.

basic Bass Workout

You should also experiment with leaving space in lines such as these.

The final example is a faster 16th-note line based on the style of the great Jaco Pastorius. This is about as relentless as these sort of lines get and you'll find it tiring for your plucking hand. You can avoid tiring your hand by making use of those phrasing techniques discussed in Chapter 8.

Exercise 10

10 SLAP BASS

Slap bass is one of the most exciting ways of playing the bass, and there are few who have picked up the instrument and not wanted to at least try it. We currently have some fantastic ambassadors for the slap technique, and indeed for the instrument itself – I'm talking about players like Flea, Fieldy, Dirk Lance, Stanley Clarke, Mark King, Victor Wooten, Stu Hamm and, of course, the daddy of slap bass, Larry Graham.

To a beginner, taking those first few tentative slaps on the bass can be quite daunting. As likely as not, the first time you try it, it will feel awkward and clumsy, and it probably won't sound that great either! However, while slapping is a very popular and funky-sounding way of playing the instrument, this doesn't necessarily mean that it has to be difficult. Remember – just because something looks and sounds difficult, it doesn't mean that it is! I'm not saying that it's easy, just that it's not as hard as you might think. It's certainly worth remembering that even the best 'slappers' struggled with their thumbs to begin with. Perseverance with the following exercises will pay off – that's one promise I can make to you. Slap bass is one of the most enjoyable styles to learn, and I can also promise that, if you're a newcomer to the style, you're going to have a blast learning it. For those of you who are already well acquainted with the technique, hopefully there will be something for you here, too.

Many people assume that slap bass is all about the thumb when in fact success with the techniques lies in the integration of both hands. While it's almost impossible to produce a string of 16th notes with the thumb alone, by using both hands to hammer out rhythms it's possible to produce twice the number of notes with half the effort. I always liken this technique to drumming on a tabletop with my hands. It's quite easy to do, and pretty much everyone can already do it. By applying that same technique to the bass, you can come up with some very funky sounds indeed.

There are three elements involved with playing slap bass. The first two – the thumb and the left hand – I've already talked about. The third element is the first or second finger of the right hand, which is used to 'pop' the string. Over the course of this chapter, we'll look at each element and learn how to apply it to the slap style.

The Thumb

We'll start in the most obvious place, with the thumb. I always advise my students to give some thought about the way in which they slap the string. This is affected mainly by the position of the bass on your body. For example, if you wear the bass low when you play, your slap technique will be very different from how it would be if you wore it higher. Consider the contrasting styles of Flea, who wears his bass low, with that of someone like Mark King, who wears his bass quite high. Flea slaps with his hand at a right angle to the string whereas Mark has his arm parallel to the strings. Both methods work and it's down to you, the player, to decide which works best for you. Personally, I prefer to wear the bass in approximately the same position as it would be if I was seated. As discussed in Chapter 4, this enables me to maintain the same angles in my arms and wrists whether I am sitting or standing, so there's minimal difference to my technique whichever I'm doing. By doing this, I'm also able to keep my thumb parallel to the strings, which makes striking the other strings besides the E a lot easier.

To begin with, try slapping the string with the side of your thumb, on the knucklebone, and aim for just over the last fret on your bass. As you strike the string, it's

basic Bass Workout

important to keep a degree of flexibility in the wrist, as relaxation will enable your thumb to bounce. This is very important in the slap sound.

In Exercise 1 we're simply going to strike the E, A and D strings of the bass. If you're wondering why you're not slapping all of the strings, it's because you rarely have to slap the G string at all. Usually, this one – and frequently the D string – will be popped by the first or second finger.

Exercise 1

You'll probably find it trickier to hit the A and D strings, as you'll have the E and A strings in the way. Remember what I said about keeping your thumb parallel to the strings – this should help you to hit the string that you want. Once you have the fundamentals of this technique under your belt, I recommend a little 'target practice', practising hitting each string in turn as accurately and cleanly as possible.

Try this with fretted notes as well:

Exercise 2

The Left Hand

The left hand is equally important in the slap bass style and not just for those funky 16th-note rhythms. As I've already mentioned, it also plays a valuable part in muting. Try slapping a G on your E string. Now lift the left-hand finger slightly after you've struck the note. The note should stop. This is a standard muting technique and is used in many styles of playing. It is, however, a very useful part of the slap style, hence its inclusion in this chapter.

In the next example I've notated a simple eighth-note bass line. By using the technique I've just explained, you can maintain a more 'staccato' feel and play a tight eighth-note groove.

Here's the same line from Exercise 2 with the muting applied to it:

basic Bass Workout

t t t t t t t *simile*

Exercise 3

If you wanted to play long notes rather than staccato notes, obviously you could simply leave your fingers in place without performing any muting. Although in this instance I've added staccato marks (those little dots below each note), this is not always written in slap notation and is frequently left to the discretion of the player.

The left hand is also responsible for creating ghost notes. By slapping the string with the left hand in the correct place you can create a ghost – or 'dead' – note that will add a percussive effect to your playing. This can be a tricky concept to grasp, but all you need to do is slap your fingers against the strings to create a 'thud'. You do, however, need to ensure that the ghost note is actually a ghost note and doesn't have any kind of pitch – hitting the strings too hard will result in a fretted note.

You also have to be careful not to play any unwanted harmonics. I've found that the best place to hit the string is roughly over the sixth fret. This fret doesn't have a strong harmonic, whereas frets 5 and 7 do.

The following exercise requires you to play a slapped note with the thumb, closely followed by a dead left-hand slap:

Exercise 4

Now try something a little faster. Imagine slapping out a 16th-note pulse with your hands on the tabletop. The next exercise follows that principle, since you'll be alternating between playing thumb slaps and left-hand slaps.

Exercise 5

basic Bass Workout

Sounds pretty tricky, I'm sure you'll agree, but the principle is very simple.

You can also play ghost notes with the thumb, simply by slapping the string as you would with any note but muting the string with the left hand. By combining ordinary slapped notes, left-hand slaps and slapped ghost notes together it's possible to produce patterns like the one in the following exercise:

Exercise 6

Things are starting to sound funkier now – it's time to add the final element to our slap-bass arsenal.

The Pop

By using the thumb and left hand in the combinations previously illustrated, we're already able to come up some rather convincing slap lines, but an integral part of the style is the popped notes that add that final bit of funk. These are played with either the first or second finger of the right hand, it doesn't matter which. In fact, it's quite useful to be able to use both, as they will come in useful for some of the more advanced slap techniques. Try hooking your finger just underneath the G string and pulling the note. Try not to use too much of your finger – you really need to pluck only with the end to produce the desired tone. Do this quite aggressively and hopefully you'll produce the same sound as that demonstrated on the CD.

Popped notes aren't much use on their own and need to be used in context with some slapped notes. A popular choice is the octave above the note you've already slapped. Try the following exercise, which mixes the two in a simple eighth-note line:

Exercise 7

By applying the muting technique discussed earlier in the chapter, you can make this sound funkier still:

Exercise 8

We've now covered the basic elements of the slap style. When combined with standard left-hand techniques such as hammer-ons, pull-offs and slides (see Chapter 8, 'Phrasing Techniques'), we can produce lines of considerable complexity.

The final five examples of this chapter are slap grooves I've written for you to practise. They vary in their level of difficulty, but by following the slap guides and using the information in this chapter you should be able to execute them perfectly. If you're new to the technique, take these slowly and carefully; there's nothing in these exercises that I haven't covered in this chapter. Hopefully you'll soon be coming up with lines like these on your own.

Exercise 9 is based around a figure which is repeated in every bar in a couple of different positions. You'll notice that I've notated staccato marks for the pops, but remember, they won't always be there:

Exercise 9

In Exercise 10 you'll need to work on your popping technique to get the feel right. Watch out for the figure in the last bar:

Exercise 10

Exercise 11 contains a *double stop*, which is where two notes are popped together. To do this, pop one with the first finger and one with the second simultaneously.

basic Bass Workout

In this instance, your first finger will be popping the F♯ on the D string and your second will be popping the D on the G string.

Exercise 11

Exercise 12 features some tricky hammer-ons and pull-offs. For the figure at the beginning of the second bar, you will see that a slur connects all five notes. This means that this group should sound as one fluid phrase. You might want to take this slowly to start with, especially if you're not used to hammering on and pulling off at speed.

Exercise 12

This last one is a bit of a monster, but I've included it as an example of what's possible with the slap technique. Once again, there's nothing here that hasn't been covered in this chapter. Be careful with this one – there are a lot of notes and some tricky rhythms to contend with. In the first bar you'll notice that again I have included the hammer-on phrase from the previous exercise, while in the second bar we have some sliding tenths. These are played simply by slapping and popping as notated, but allowing the notes to ring into each other, creating a chordal effect.

In the third bar there is the same effect but with octaves.

Exercise 13

Finally, one of the most important aspects about learning something new is getting out there and listening to as much of it as you can. Check out the guys who are using this technique and see if you can work out what they're doing. Studying any of the players mentioned at the beginning of the chapter will be enormously beneficial to your slap playing, and there are many more 'slappers' out there that I haven't mentioned.

11 USING A PICK

Playing the bass with a pick is something that for many years has mainly been the practice of rock musicians. There are a few possible explanations for this. Firstly, playing with a pick produces a heavier, punchier sound than playing with the fingers. This is because the attack that is produced by the plastic of the plectrum striking the string cannot be reproduced with the tips of the fingers. Secondly, many rock bassists seem to have started out as guitarists, and since 95 per cent of rock guitar playing is done with a pick, it makes sense to use a pick on the bass as well. It's also a more aggressive style of playing, one that you can literally put your entire arm into – especially if you wear your bass low. You might also notice pick players wearing sweatbands on their wrists, particularly the picking hand. This is mainly to protect the skin from the constant abrasion against the edge of the bass or the bridge.

Playing with a pick has its advantages and disadvantages over fingerstyle playing, all of which will hopefully become obvious throughout this chapter.

basic Bass Workout

The pick is usually held between the first finger and thumb of the right hand. As you pluck the strings, it's helpful to rest the wrist of your right hand on either the bridge or body of the bass – this provides a stable anchor point from which to play. There are many different ways to play using a pick – some bassists, for example, will use mostly downstrokes (an approach favoured by Jason Newsted of Metallica) while others use a combination of down- and upstrokes. Whether you use just downstrokes or a combination of both depends mainly on the tempo – at slow tempos it's relatively easy to use just downstrokes, but at fast tempos of 140 beats per minute upwards you're going to need both. I recommend practising using both downstrokes and upstrokes – it will enable you to play cleaner and faster.

Let's look at some exercises that will help you to develop your pick playing. In all of following exercises I have added guides for upstrokes and downstrokes:

Downstroke = ⊓   Upstroke = V

In Exercise 1 we're simply going to play eighth notes, using up- and downstrokes. Try to keep all the notes even and maintain the same volume whichever way you're picking:

Exercise 1

In Exercise 2 we will play a more active bass part that will require you to cross strings. Try to keep the line sounding smooth as much as possible – when playing with a pick it can be all too easy for your playing to start to sound disjointed.

Exercise 2

Now let's take a look at one of those 16th-note parts discussed earlier. For now, we'll keep to a reasonable tempo, such as 100 beats per minute. With lines like these it can be tricky to cross strings soundlessly, so make sure you have the line sounding good at a slow tempo before speeding things up.

basic Bass Workout

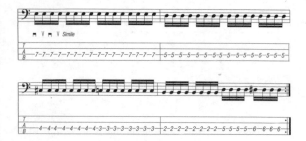

Exercise 3

As I said earlier, the main disadvantage with using a pick is that it's very difficult to jump from string to string. Moving from one string to the next – from the E to the A, for example – doesn't normally present a problem, but if you were required to play a line that jumped continuously from the E to the D (or G), you would experience considerable difficulty. This perhaps explains why pick playing isn't used in many genres other than rock music.

12 TRANSCRIBING

Transcribing other bass players' lines is a valuable part of your ear training. As a bass player, you're seeking to find your own voice on the instrument. The best way to do this is to absorb as much music as you can and learn from players that you admire. Transcribing other bass players' parts helps you to learn their styles, their note choices, and encourages you to think in new ways. When you transcribe a lot of material by the same artist, you'll get into their mindset – you'll start to make accurate guesses at how things were played or conceived.

Transcribing and learning from a wide variety of bassists, each of whom play in differing styles, will do wonders for your playing. To craft your own style, you must first assimilate the styles of others. It all sounds very *Star Trek*, but it's a fact. Jaco would never have sounded like Jaco had he not spent years learning soul and Motown tunes, assimilating the work of Jamerson, Jerry Jemmot, Duck Dunn, transcribing Charlie Parker's sax lines and learning and studying melodies.

Reading Music

It helps a great deal if you can read music, as it stands to reason that if you know how to read something you should be able to write it down. I learnt to read by learning to write music, so I guess I took the backwards approach! However, being able to write out your transcriptions in notation doesn't mean that you have to. I'll often use a combination of notation and tablature – essentially tablature with rhythms attached. The benefit of doing so means that I'm able to notate rhythms and represent the easiest fingerings and note placings in one go.

Speeding It Up

Now, you might be thinking that there can be no benefit whatsoever to speeding up something you're transcribing. After all, speeding it up will only make it harder, right? Wrong – at least partly. Speeding a song up allows the bass part to 'pop' out of the mix. I use this technique a lot on tracks where the bass part is buried in the mix. Go ahead and try it and you'll see what I mean. Find a tape player with a high-speed dubbing facility, preferably an old one you don't mind messing about with. Put a blank tape in the record deck and your song in the play deck. Record the track on high-speed dubbing – you'll hear the bass jump out of the mix. (Note: If you don't want to waste a blank tape, you can sometimes fool old tape machines by manually depressing the recording tabs inside the record deck.) Besides giving a more audible bass part (albeit with Chipmunks-style vocals attached), one of the benefits of doing this is that the speeded-up track sounds roughly an octave above the normal pitch of your bass. You may have to make some minor tuning adjustments to your bass but I'd be surprised if it varied more than a semitone. This technique is best used for tracks that have relatively simple bass lines, and if they're too fast for you to play, you should be able to hum what you hear and then translate this to your bass.

This technique can also be demonstrated by playing a 45rpm record at 75rpm.

Slowing It Down

In the days before digital technology, I would slow tracks down by using karaoke machines or four-track recorders and then detune my bass appropriately. It worked, but it was frustrating. These days we don't have to do that, as the technology exists to slow down audio without altering the pitch – another of the luxuries we enjoy today, but one I embrace heartily!

You can do this yourself through a computer using the numerous bits of software that will enable you to *time-shift*, as the process is known. (Sounding distinctly sci-fi again, isn't it?) Alternatively, there are headphone amplifiers for bass on the market that also offer this feature, and even the latest version of Windows Media Player can do it. The advantage of using such a device is that what you're hearing is slower but the pitch hasn't altered. It's therefore easier for your ear to cope with and you won't need to detune your bass.

Looping

Computers can be an amazing help when you're transcribing, and no, it's not cheating to use them! I find it useful sometimes to loop a small section of the tune I'm transcribing. (Again, there are plenty of audio programs out there that will do this for you.) This means that you hear only the part you need to, around and around.

Sing It Back

As I said, you need to stop the track after the note or notes you're working out. Being able to sing them after you've just heard them is just as essential. If you can sing them a couple of times, it shouldn't take too long for you to locate those same notes on your instrument.

Keeping A Notepad

As I mentioned in Chapter 4, it's always useful to keep a music pad around for when you want to write ideas down. This is equally important for transcribing. I keep a large A4 pad of manuscript paper purely for transcribing music – and it doesn't take long for me to fill it up.

Transcribing A Whole Piece

In many instances you won't want to transcribe an entire song, maybe just a lick or a fill you want to borrow, but sometimes you'll need to do the whole thing from start to finish. When doing so, I recommend a little preparation. First of all, listen through, pen and paper in hand, and sketch out the structure of the song on score paper – verses, choruses, middle eight, solos and so on. Try to draw in bar lines so that you basically have a blank chart to fill in. Look out for repetition – most songs use the same format and chord progression for each verse and chorus.

13 BUYING A BASS

Whether you're buying your first bass, upgrading to a better model or having a bass custom-made, there are a few important considerations. In this chapter, I'll look at the three ranges of instruments – entry-level, mid-range and high-end – and try to offer some tips and advice that will help you to make a purchase.

General

Without question, you should try a bass before you buy it. If you're a complete beginner, you may wonder what possible benefit trying a bass can have, since you might not be able to play anything! Nevertheless, it's important to sit with the bass and hold it, see how it feels, perhaps try some different models and compare them. Here's a list of general things to look for:

- Good balance. The headstock on some cheaper basses will dive straight towards the floor when you let go, which means that you'll be forever holding the bass up, having to work harder to play it.

- Weight. A bass that's too heavy is going to put strain on your back if you wear it while standing for too long.

- A smooth, comfortable neck, with no sharp fret ends that might hurt your fingers.

- Good construction, with a smooth, unblemished finish.

- Most importantly, how does it sound?

Entry-Level Basses: £100–£350

So, you've decided to play the bass guitar. Now all you need to do is buy one. It's possible to buy an entry-level bass guitar for as little as £100, but it's often worth spending a little more if you can. Obviously, the more you spend, the more you get for your money – and generally speaking, buying a bass isn't going to require you to sell a kidney! Basses in the low-budget range are getting better all the time, and it's now possible to get your hands on a very nice instrument for your money. More and more basses are now available with active electronics, something that used to be the domain purely of mid-range and high-end instruments, and where possible you should get a bass with an active circuit. Some basses also allow you to switch between active and passive modes.

Also, just because you're buying an entry-level bass doesn't mean that it can't look good. As the bass grows in popularity, more and more manufacturers are building instruments that are not only affordable but look good, too.

As far as construction goes, many basses in this range are made out of basswood or alder, both very common choices. It's always a good thing if the bass has a finish that allows you to see the wood grain, since that will mean that it's not made out of plywood. Don't laugh – some low-range basses are made of plywood and then painted and lacquered to disguise the fact.

Most necks are made from maple and fingerboards from rosewood, both of which are perfectly satisfactory choices. In this range you'll find that all of the instruments will be mass-produced, assembly-line basses.

Some excellent entry-level basses are made by Cort, Tanglewood, Peavey, Yamaha and Squier (by Fender).

Mid-Range Basses: £400–£1,200
I've called this category the 'upgrade bass', as this is the sort of money you're likely to spend on your second instrument.

By now you'll probably have been playing for a couple of years and are probably wanting to get yourself a better instrument. Once you've decided to upgrade, or even start with a mid-range bass, you have a few more options. There are now many companies renowned for building high-spec basses that are offering mid-range instruments in an attempt to reach what is without a doubt the biggest slice of the bass market. You'll find that active electronics are commonplace within this price range and through-neck designs are available – even from the lower end of the range. There are also considerably more options wood-/finish-wise than before.

Some recommended basses in the lower part of the mid-range are made by Yamaha, Cort, Bass Collection, Aria, Ibanez and Fender, most of whom also manufacture basses in the upper mid-range as well. In the upper mid-range we have Warwick, MusicMan, MTD and Status.

High-End Basses: £1,200+

I've called this category the 'dream' category, since for many people, when they invest a considerable amount of money in a high-end instrument, it's one that they regard as their personal holy grail of basses, and one they will keep hold of.

basic Bass Workout

This category again divides into a couple of subcategories. Firstly, you'll be able to walk into a shop and buy a high-spec bass straight off the wall. These basses will be built by well-known and well-established companies able to produce instruments in larger numbers than independent luthiers. You'll find that, if the bass you see isn't exactly what you want, there will usually be a full range of custom options available, including different colours and finishes, string configurations, hardware and pick-ups and electronics.

In the high-end category we also have instruments built by independent luthiers. These will be instruments built by very skilled craftsmen able to produce stunning woodworking and instruments of exceptional and personal quality. You won't see quite so many of these in the shops, since for the most part each instrument will have been produced for a specific customer.

Talking to an experienced luthier you can choose your options from the outset, by specifying exotic woods for body, neck and fingerboard, colours and finishes, and custom options – even some that you've thought of yourself.

Basses in this range include those by Yamaha, Alembic, Status, Zon, Tobias, Sei, GB, Ken Smith, Pedulla and Fodera.